MR. MEN™ LITTLE MISS™ © THOIP (a SANRIO company)

Mr Grumpy Nails Fatherhood © 2018 THOIP (a SANRIO company)
Printed and published under licence from Price Stern Sloan, Inc., Los Angeles.
Published in Great Britain by Egmont UK Limited
The Yellow Building, 1 Nicholas Road, London W11 4AN

ISBN 978 1 4052 9191 0
68268/1
Printed in Italy

MR. GRUMPY
NAILS
FATHERHOOD

Roger Hargreaves

Original concept and illustrations by
Roger Hargreaves

Written by
Sarah Daykin, Lizzie Daykin and Liz Bankes

EGMONT

This is Mr Grumpy. Mr Grumpy is a dad. Now, I know what you're thinking, but Mr Grumpy is no grumpy dad.

Having three kids hasn't changed him at all.

I mean, yes, his daughter refuses to be seen in public with him. And yes, he thinks 'Bae' is some sort of herb. But he still knows how to party! Even if parties now involve pass the parcel, party bags and children being sick.

It wasn't all plain sailing of course – fatherhood doesn't come with instructions. And if it did, he wouldn't read them anyway.

It was another normal Saturday morning. *Creak* went the bedroom door, *pitter patter* went the tiny feet, *OUCH!* went Mr Grumpy, as the toddler shoved a Lego brick up his nose.

Time to get up and ferry the kids to their long list of clubs, parties and play-dates, while his wife locked herself in the spare room for her fortnightly lie-in.

But really, how hard could it be? It was just like being a taxi driver. If your passengers didn't pay you, made you play the same song on repeat and wrote rude words on the car window.

First he dropped the 8-year-old at Annabel's VIP Princess Party. He'd forgotten to buy a present and hoped Annabel had put 'a multipack of crisps from the petrol station' on her wish list.

Next stop trampolining, but only after a tense negotiation with the 4-year-old, where she insisted on wearing her Teenage Mutant Ninja Turtle costume under her leotard. Followed by swimming, where she insisted on wearing jeans.

Finally, he did the family shop and bought an armful of groceries. And despite losing three eggs and a head of broccoli along the way, he was still glad he'd saved the 5p by refusing a bag.

Still plenty of time to get lots of stuff done thought Mr Grumpy.

Instead he spent the next three hours looking for Boo-Boo, a germ-infested blanky with a life of its own.

And he completely ran out of time to put that blimmin' shelf up.

A while later, after the kids' twentieth game of 'Sledging Down the Stairs in a Washing Basket', Mr Grumpy suggested a brand new game called 'Close Your Eyes and Don't Move or Speak'.

It turned out that Mr Grumpy was especially good at this one, and was just nodding off when he heard the sound of the letterbox.

'That's odd,' he thought, 'bit late for the postman …'

When the toddler had been retrieved from next door's hedge, Mr Grumpy handed over duties to his wife and commenced his important weekend appointment of sitting on the loo and playing a game on his phone for an hour.

His wife knocked to ask if he'd found a portal to another world.

'You never let me have ANYTHING!' screamed his daughter, when he finally emerged. 'Annabel's parents bought her a phone AND a laptop AND they let her live in virtual reality.'

'Now listen here young lady,' said Mr Grumpy. 'In my day, I was happy playing with a cardboard box!'

But suddenly Mr Grumpy realised what he was saying …

I *AM* A GRUMPY DAD!

Mr Grumpy couldn't believe it. Something had to be done. He sent a message to the Mr Men Dads' WhatsApp group.

MR. GRUMPY
Lads! Who's free for a pint?

MR. WORRY
Sorry, I can't. I've got to finish my child's school project.

MR. BUMP
Sorry, I can't. I tried to join in with my son's football match and I think I have a hernia.

MR. MUDDLE
Sorry, I can't. I've got to put that blimmin' shelf up.

None of the others replied, so he called Mr Mean.

'Sorry I didn't get back to you, I'm a bit tied up at the moment,' said Mr Mean.

'Oh should I call back later?' said Mr Grumpy.

'No, I've literally been tied up – the kids have staged a coup. They're revolting against tidying their rooms.'

'What are their demands this time?' said Mr Grumpy.

'Ten thousand pounds and a puppy,' said Mr Mean. 'Anyway, I'll try my best to come out. Just need to find a babysitter – the last three won't return my calls.'

Mr Grumpy called Mr Clever.

'I'd love to join you,' he said, 'but I've got to put the fear of God into my daughter's new boyfriend this weekend.'

'How are you going to do that?' asked Mr Grumpy.

'Take him to one side and ask him how he plans to provide for her. Then challenge him to an arm wrestle.'

'Well that seems … How old is he?'

'Eight.'

Mr Grumpy wasn't getting very far, so he decided to try Mr Cool. Mr Cool didn't have children, he just had freedom and a disposable income.

'Hey!' said Mr Cool. 'I'm just flying my private jet over the Andes. Going for brunch at this great new pop-up.'

'I can't get anyone to come out,' moaned Mr Grumpy.

'That's because you're thinking too small,' said Mr Cool. 'What you guys need is an EPIC, SPONTANEOUS, LEGENDARY NIGHT OUT!'

'An epic night out?' thought Mr Grumpy. They hadn't done that for years. Not since Magaluf and the Curious Incident of Mr Silly and the Inflatable Banana in the Night-time.

Three months later, when Mr Mean had finally found a babysitter, it was time for the night out to commence.

Mr Grumpy was just trying to leave the house for the second time (after his first shirt had been affectionately decorated by a jammy-fingered toddler) when his 8-year-old cornered him.

'Dad! What do mermaids eat? Why am I pink and you're blue? Where do babies come from?'

'Um … ask your mother,' said Mr Grumpy.

'I did! She said to ask you.'

Mr Grumpy arrived twenty minutes late, but luckily all the Mr Dads were still outside the bar, taking it in turns to touch Mr Cool's car.

'Do you think you can fit a booster seat in there?' said Mr Daydream hopefully.

It was good to see the lads again. Yes, there were a few more beer guts. And a few more grey hairs. Mr Forgetful's hair had receded all the way to the back of his neck, but his hat did an excellent job of hiding it.

They hit the dance floor and pulled out all the classics: the Lawnmower, the Sprinkler, the Robot, the Running Man, the Stumbling Man, the Falling Over Man, and the Too Old To Be In This Club Man.

It was 11pm and Mr Cool went to get another round.

'Great!' said Mr Grumpy, as his dreams of bed faded and he wondered if the bar would serve him a tea.

'I probably need to go if I'm going to make the last train,' said Mr Good.

'I think I need to go to hospital,' said Mr Bump, nursing his hernia.

'Shall we have a little sit-down?' said Mr Lazy.

Mr Cool returned from the bar, and what do you think he saw?

All the Mr Dads were having a nap!

They'd completely missed the table dancer.

And when Mr Mean was asked to leave for 'aggressive snoring', it was time to call it a night.

'I'm staying out, losers!' laughed Mr Cool.

He wasn't tired at all, he loved overcrowded clubs with really loud music, and he didn't fancy going back to his empty flat just yet.

Mr Grumpy was outside the house for an hour before finally managing to get the key in the lock. He tiptoed quietly into the hallway, tripped over Boo-Boo and fell head first into a miniature drum kit. The night had been fun, but he was relieved to be home. And it was nice to see the kids, particularly as they were fast asleep.

Creak, went his bedroom door the next morning. 'Do you want to hang out?' said his daughter. 'We can listen to that rubbish music you like and play with a cardboard box if you want?'

And so they did. For a bit. Then they played on the PlayStation because it was more fun.

Perhaps it's not so bad being a grumpy dad, thought Mr Grumpy. In fact there was only one thing that would make this day more perfect …

'See you in a few hours!' he called, as he grabbed his phone and went to sit on the loo.